Zac Efron

ABDO
Publishing Company

A Big Buddy Book
by **Sarah Tieck**

VISIT US AT
www.abdopublishing.com

Published by ABDO Publishing Company, 8000 West 78th Street, Edina, Minnesota 55439.

Printed in the United States.

Coordinating Series Editor: Rochelle Baltzer
Contributing Editors: Heidi M.D. Elston, Megan M. Gunderson, Marcia Zappa
Graphic Design: Maria Hosley
Cover Photograph: AP Photo: Tammie Arroyo
Interior Photographs/Illustrations: AP Photo: Stephen Chernin (page 15), Kevork Djensezian (page 26), Richard Drew (pages 23, 27), Luis Martinez (page 11), Chris Pizzello (pages 5, 20, 23, 25), Matt Sayles (pages 14, 29), Dan Steinberg (page 9); FilmMagic.com: Michael Rozman (page 17); Getty Images: Bryan Bedder (page 13), Charley Gallay (page 7), Frazer Harrison (page 10), WireImage/Eric Neitzel (page 19), WireImage/John Sciulli (page 21).

Library of Congress Cataloging-in-Publication Data

Tieck, Sarah, 1976-
 Zac Efron / Sarah Tieck.
    p. cm. -- (Big buddy biographies)
 Includes index.
 ISBN 978-1-60453-120-6
 1. Efron, Zac--Juvenile literature. 2. Actors--United States--Biography--Juvenile literature. I. Title.

PN2287.E395T54 2009
792.02'8092--dc22
 [B]
                                 2008011384

Contents

A Rising Star

Zac Efron is an actor and a singer. He has appeared in television shows and movies. Zac is most famous for starring in *High School Musical* and *Hairspray*.

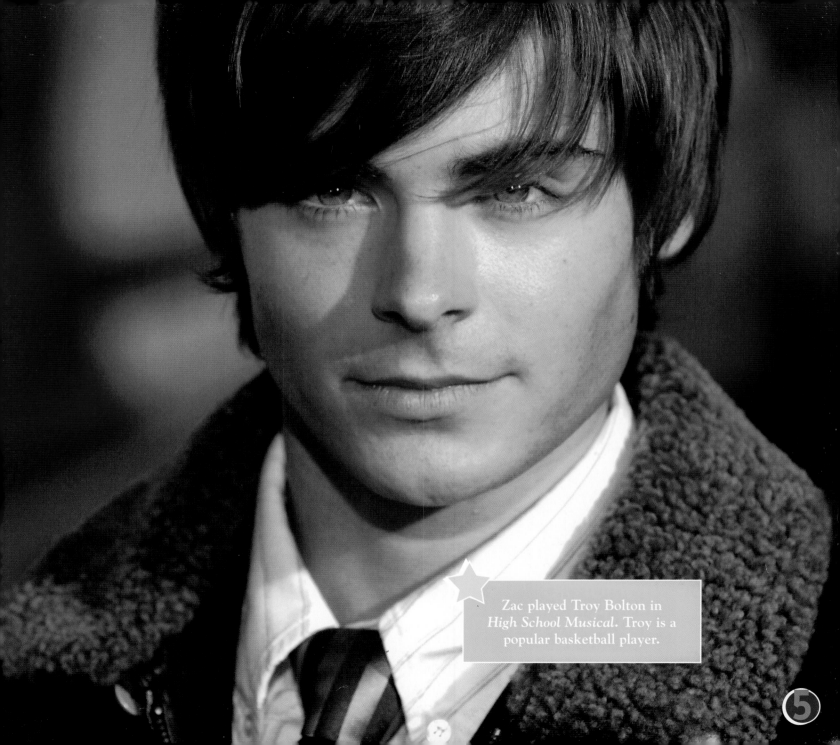

Zac played Troy Bolton in *High School Musical*. Troy is a popular basketball player.

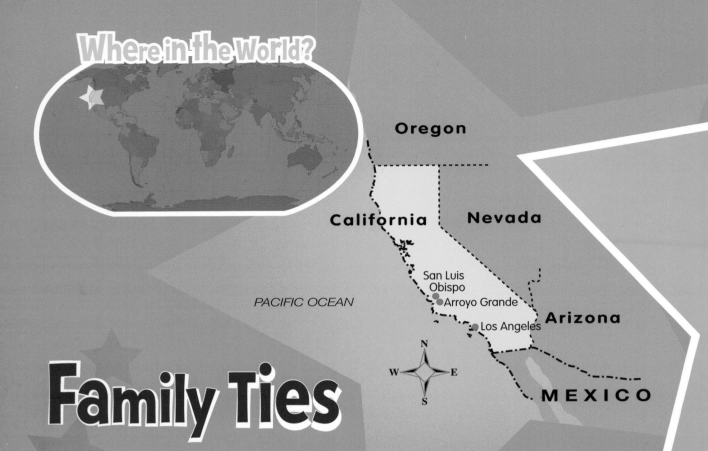

Oregon

California

Nevada

San Luis
Obispo

Arroyo Grande

PACIFIC OCEAN

Los Angeles

Arizona

N
W   E
S

MEXICO

Family Ties

Zachary David Alexander "Zac" Efron was born on October 18, 1987, in San Luis Obispo, California. His parents are Starla Baskett and David Efron. Zac has one younger brother named Dylan.

Sometimes Zac's parents attend events with him.

Growing Up

Zac grew up on California's central coast. He and his family lived in a small beach town called Arroyo Grande. There, Zac attended local schools. And, his parents worked for a local power company. David was an **engineer**, and Starla was a **secretary**.

Zac worked hard at school. But when his homework was done, he liked to play video games. Playing video games is still one of Zac's favorite hobbies.

A Young Actor

When Zac was young, his parents noticed his natural talent for performing. He could copy dancing he saw and singing he heard. After watching *The Wizard of Oz*, he danced like the Tin Man. And when Zac heard songs on the radio, he could sing them back.

Other people noticed Zac's talent, too. In eighth grade, Zac took a theater class. He was so good, his teacher said he should become an actor!

Zac took voice and piano lessons to improve his talents. Then, he began **auditioning** for **musicals** and plays.

Zac appeared in several **productions** in his community. His first part was at age 11. Zac played a newsboy in the musical *Gypsy*. Soon, he was performing regularly.

Zac says singing is not his strength.
Still, he has performed in many musicals.

13

Starting Out

Zac wanted to become a television or movie actor. So, his mom drove him to Los Angeles, California, for **auditions**.

At first, Zac did not have much success. Then in 2002, he got a few small parts. Zac appeared in the television shows *Firefly*, *ER*, and *The Guardian*.

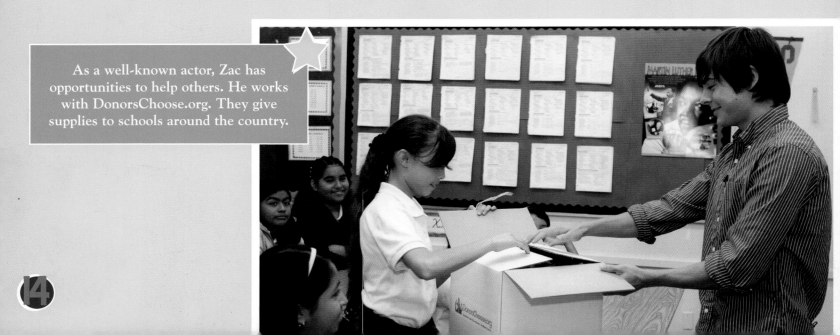

As a well-known actor, Zac has opportunities to help others. He works with DonorsChoose.org. They give supplies to schools around the country.

Zac's popularity grew. Soon, he appeared on television shows such as *Total Request Live*.

In 2004, Zac starred in a television movie called *Miracle Run*. He played an **autistic** boy named Steven.

That same year, Zac got a part on *Summerland*. He appeared regularly on this television series as Cameron Bale. This job taught Zac about life as a **professional** actor.

Zac gained important experience working with the cast of *Summerland*.

Did you know...

Zac has a low singing voice. Many *High School Musical* songs were written for a higher voice. Because of this, another singer helped sing some of the songs.

Big Break

Zac's big break came when he **auditioned** for the Disney Channel movie *High School Musical*. His singing, dancing, and acting skills made him stand out! Zac got one of the lead parts.

Corbin Bleu, Vanessa Hudgens, Zac, and Ashley Tisdale starred in *High School Musical*. They became good friends while working on the movie.

In *High School Musical*, Zac's character falls in love with Vanessa's character.

*High School **Musical*** first appeared on the Disney Channel in 2006. It was an instant success. Zac and the show's other stars became famous!

In 2006, the cast of *High School Musical* won an Emmy Award for their work. The Academy of Television Arts and Sciences gives these awards to the year's best television programs, writers, and actors. Since then, Zac has also won Kids' Choice Awards and Teen Choice Awards.

High School Musical

*High School **Musical*** is one of the Disney Channel's most successful movies. In it, Zac's character, Troy, **auditions** for the school musical. He falls in love with a girl named Gabriella. Another girl, Sharpay, works to keep them both out of the musical.

The cast of *High School Musical* has appeared in magazines and on television. Fans can purchase numerous products connected with the movie. These include clothes, toys, books, albums, and DVDs.

In April 2006, the stars of *High School Musical* performed on the *Today* show.

New Opportunities

After his work on *High School Musical*, Zac had new opportunities. Some of his songs became big hits! And, he starred in more movies. In 2007, he was in *High School Musical 2*.

High School Musical 2 celebrated its opening at Disneyland in California.

One of Zac's favorite parts was Link Larkin in *Hairspray*. Zac did all the singing for this part. And, he was able to work with many famous actors. John Travolta, Michelle Pfeiffer, Christopher Walken, and Queen Latifah all starred in *Hairspray*. The movie first appeared in 2007.

In *Hairspray,* Nikki Blonsky played Tracy Turnblad.
Tracy becomes a dancer and helps change the world.
Zac played a dancer who falls in love with her.

27

Buzz

After *Hairspray*, Zac moved to Los Angeles. In 2008, he worked on several movies. Zac had a part in *Seventeen Again*. He also appeared in *High School **Musical** 3: Senior Year*. This movie first appeared in theaters rather than on television!

Zac wants to continue acting. He plans to work on more musicals. One day, Zac would like to star in movies as an action hero!

Did you know...

Zac would like to attend the University of Southern California to study film.

Snapshot

★ **Name**: Zachary David Alexander Efron

★**Birthday**: October 18, 1987

★**Birthplace**: San Luis Obispo, California

★**Home**: Los Angeles, California

★**Appearances**: *Miracle Run, Summerland, High School Musical, Hairspray, High School Musical 2, Seventeen Again, High School Musical 3: Senior Year*

Important Words

audition (aw-DIH-shuhn) to give a trial performance showcasing personal talent as a musician, a singer, a dancer, or an actor.

autism (AW-tih-zuhm) a brain disorder that begins in childhood and affects development. A person who has autism is autistic.

engineer (ehn-jih-NEER) a person who is trained to apply scientific knowledge to a practical purpose such as building machines or buildings.

musical a story told with music.

production a performance such as a play, a television show, or a movie.

professional (pruh-FEHSH-nuhl) working for money rather than for pleasure.

secretary a person whose work is keeping records for a company.

Web Sites

To learn more about Zac Efron, visit ABDO Publishing Company on the World Wide Web. Web sites about Zac Efron are featured on our Book Links page. These links are routinely monitored and updated to provide the most current information available.

www.abdopublishing.com

Index